History of Joseph, Dad of Jesus

by

Joseph P. Messina

Table of Contents

Dedication

To Mary, Mother of Jesus, whose unwavering faith and grace serve as a source of inspiration for this work. Your presence in the hearts of believers echoes through the generations, guiding all who seek love and divine truth.

Acknowledgment

I would like to express my deepest gratitude to Mary, Mother of Jesus, for the inspiration she has provided throughout the creation of this work. Her strength, humility, and divine presence have been a constant guide, shaping not only the history of Joseph but also the spirit in which this narrative has been written.

Chapter 1: History of Joseph

Joseph, often referred to as the earthly father of Jesus, is a significant figure in Christian tradition. He was a carpenter by trade and lived in Nazareth. According to the Gospels of Matthew and Luke, Joseph was a descendant of King David, fulfilling the prophecy that the Messiah would come from David's lineage. Joseph was betrothed to Mary when he learned of her miraculous pregnancy. An angel appeared to him in a dream, assuring him that the child was conceived by the Holy Spirit and instructing him to take Mary as his wife. Joseph obeyed, demonstrating his faith and humility

He played a protective role in Jesus' early life. For instance, he fled with Mary and Jesus to Egypt to escape King Herod's decree to kill all male infants in Bethlehem. After Herod's death, Joseph brought his family back to Nazareth. Although not much is known about Joseph's later life, he is remembered as a man of integrity, faith, and obedience to God's will. His role as a father figure to Jesus and a supportive husband to Mary highlights his importance in the biblical narrative.

Mary first met Joseph when she was twelve years old. Joseph was at the temple for his Bar Mitzvah, a ceremony marking his acceptance as a man into the community of faith. Attracted to his physical maturity, she invited him to dine at their table. Mary was nine, and the tradition of sharing allowed her to participate. Thereafter, Joseph took his meals at the home of Joakim and Ann. Mary grew fond of him and often walked with him after the Sabbath, ever at his side. One such time, as they walked, they were approached by an inebriated guard who put his hands on Mary. Joseph pulled the man away and thrust him to the ground. Others with the guard accused Joseph of a violent attack, failing to mention their companion's condition or behavior toward Mary. From that time on, a search was made for Joseph.

Their intent to wed was formally announced according to the law, granting them liberty in the events that followed as the Holy Spirit gave life to the womb of Mary. Jesus, with Mary, visited Elizabeth, who had conceived John, the precursor of Jesus. Elizabeth recognized the holy presence within Mary's womb. The time spent there helped determine the moment for Mary and Joseph's marriage, for Mary would be showing upon their return to Jerusalem. During this period, Joseph took up thatching work while they lived with Elizabeth until she gave birth to John, whose father was Zechariah, a temple priest. Mary and Joseph then returned to their home near Jerusalem. Joseph, trained in furniture craft, advanced in his work even as the authorities continued their search. Mary spent her days with Ann, mother and daughter, sharing the changes as Jesus grew in Mary's womb.

Mary recalled the birth of John, when Zechariah finally spoke his name. When asked, he replied, "His name is John." All were astonished, for Zechariah had been unable to speak throughout Elizabeth's pregnancy. The story was retold many times, and John became a legend before his time. Perhaps that story, and having a priest for a father, inspired John to teach the laws of the Lord even as a child. John practiced baptism by word and water for all and spoke strongly of sin, naming poor parenting as the greatest failing. Joseph, with his own stories from carpentry, often joked about the mix of wood and water, and how even the stains of daily life fade with time.

Music filled their days, though the village had only one piano for more than thirty artists. Each day, residents and guests were offered an hour of entertainment. Jesus could hear the piano and would stir at its rhythm, prompting Mary to attend each day. One evening, officials announced a renewed search for Joseph during the recital. Jesus sensed Mary's distress and joined her in reacting to it. Joseph soon entered with a neighbor who carried a violin. The man joined the pianist and calmed both Mary and Jesus. Afterwards, Joseph discussed his plan to register in Bethlehem. Mary responded, "I trust in God and in Joseph."

The next morning, Mary sat upon an ass with their belongings strapped behind her, the support relieving the strain on her lower back. The journey to Bethlehem took the entire day. The city overwhelmed them upon arrival, and they could find no room. Joseph appealed to his heritage, and one man answered, "I will take you to a place where you may stay until you find what you need." He led them to an animal shelter hewn from rock, with wooden stalls built at the front. The space held animals, straw for bedding, and a manger that would later serve as a crib. Mary sighed as Joseph arranged everything they needed. Then her labor began. The barkeeper escorting them said, "My wife is a wet nurse. She will help deliver your son."

Zena, the wet nurse, had come from South Africa to live in Promise Land and was a convert to the faith. "In ten years, I have never buried a baby," she said, smiling as she wiped Mary's face, reading her expression in a very short time. With hot water she washed Mary and propped her head and back. "The Lord is my power and my pay. I deliver God's children into the world," she repeated over and over. Jesus heard her sing and came out of the darkness to hear more clearly. "I deliver God's children into the world."

"This way," she said as she clipped the cord, then cleaned the fullness of him. Drawing the sinuses clear with straws of grass at her lip, she began to sing again. Joseph brought a cloth, and she laid him on it and wiped all of him, her hands spreading olive oil everywhere. Then she toweled Jesus and sang, "My Lord, to You a son is born," as if she already knew.

Night turned to day. Shepherds with lambs on their shoulders arrived, confessing that angels had sent them. They came to see the infant who would be the king of all. The day was busy with visitors, and Mary nursed him without distress. Joseph listened to many tell of Herod ordering the death of infants. Going off in search of a caravan, Zena tended to Mary.

Joseph was directed to the Hebrew campus, where he found the caravan register for travel to Egypt. The schedule posted indicated a final destination of Alexandria. They would be out of Bethlehem in days, in Egypt within a week, at Port Said in a month, and eventually in Alexandria. They planned one day to return and live in Nazareth, beyond the time of Herod. On the west side of the campus was a large administrative tent for public screening. Angrim Shears was Sergeant of Arms. He recorded the bid to enter and was responsible for wagon space and horses within the caravan. Shears accepted Joseph's gold ring as security. They would have two days to prepare.

Many came and went, and as Joseph returned, three kings joined him and Mary. They dined together as Zena and her husband Himan set a table in the empty stall. There they shared rabbit and wine with dark, crusty bread. The kings presented their gifts for Jesus—gold, frankincense, and myrrh—and took their leave, avoiding Herod.

God sent an epiphany, for they harbored no fault. Then Zena came to say, "Himan sends me to you. But I must return to him at the border of Egypt. He will care for all your animals. There are many now, for they gained the privilege of seeing Jesus." Zena picked up Jesus and placed him in Joseph's arms. Joseph embraced him and gave him to Mary. Jesus was hungry.

They gathered what they had brought and what had been given by those nearby, packing bundles for the donkey Mary would ride to the Hebrew campus. The remaining items Joseph would give to Himan. They would take their place in the caravan that evening. Zena, Mary, and Jesus went to the hotel for bathing. It would be their last until the two-day stop at Port Said. Joseph went to the smelter to fit two gold rings and to replace the ring he had given as security for their caravan space, horses, and covered wagon. He thanked God and the three kings God had sent. The smelter already knew he was coming; all was prepared for the gold to be smelted, cast, cooled, and polished before engraving. The man's ring was named Samson, the boy's ring Barabbas.

Crossing the town center, they turned east onto Said Road, which would lead them to the campus and the caravan. On the way, Joseph killed a mad dog, winning the esteem of Zena and others. When they arrived, Himan greeted them. An excited Zena recounted the brief story of Joseph and the salivating animal. "The dog ran at Joseph, and as it leapt into the air toward him, Joseph stepped forward and thrust his arm down the dog's throat. He pulled the insides of the dog from the stomach to the jaw. Moments later, the dog dropped to the ground, dead." Zena threw her arms around Joseph and embraced him, to his embarrassment.

Himan took Joseph aside and said, "You will be with us to Alexandria. I ask you to join us in security. There is a team of four; you will make five. The authority is overall." Joseph agreed, and the men embraced. The others were at the front, setting the first three wagons. All would travel separated by the full distance of one wagon. If they fell behind schedule, they would also travel after dark. Joseph's wagon would be third from the last of the twenty.

Mary, Zena, and Jesus were already at the wagon. When Joseph joined them, he shared the security plan, including the possibility of traveling in darkness. He took Jesus from Mary, finding him wide awake. Jesus acted as if he knew Joseph and appreciated him, a pleasant surprise. Zena and Mary arranged the wagon as a residence, even a home now that Jesus was with them. Upstream of the wagons, Joseph carried Jesus, meeting neighbors and introducing him. Jesus was attentive and surprisingly participative, just as he had been active in the womb.

The five-man security team met Jesus, and instructions were built around the first wagon leaving just after daylight, with others departing before the lead team was fully out of sight. Once all were moving, security would ride horseback between every fourth wagon. Zena handled communication for Joseph. After making Jesus comfortable, Mary joined Zena, sharing much as they realized they were moving far too slowly.

Security pushed to increase travel time, and drivers closed the gaps between wagons. The improved pace offered comfort and allowed lost time to be regained. The first day came under control as daylight softened into darkness. Winter nights grew longer until March. Joseph hoped to reach Egypt by the following nightfall, to escape Herod's reach, fourteen hundred years after the death of Moses. Many kings had sought to elevate themselves as gods and had fallen from favor, beginning with Saul.

They pressed forward, but the record of Joseph's actions weakens after their arrival in Egypt until Herod's death and the family's return to Nazareth outside Jerusalem, where life became safer for the Holy Family. What followed in Nazareth was the inspiration that shaped Jesus, beyond the famous moment when he was found in the temple "going about his Father's business."

Joseph remained serious in his duties, repeatedly touring the line of wagons. Strangers blended with tenants as they made camp in the darkness. The other security members dismissed concerns, seeing nothing unusual. Joseph, still on edge, joined wagon four, where the Simon family—parents with five teenage sons—and several local boys were gathered. The locals threatened the Simons. Joseph, unseen until he stepped forward, ordered them to leave. They defiantly replied, "No." With six to one odds, they felt falsely confident. Joseph stepped between the two tallest boys and told them again to leave. Again, they answered, "No." Grabbing the two by the neck, he pushed them forward. They offered no resistance, stumbling to stay upright. After ten feet, all shouted, "We are going!" They fled, and the Simons were left surprised. Joseph advised them to sleep but wake before daylight.

Joseph returned to the wagon. Mary sat beside Jesus, and Zena beside Mary, helping keep them warm. Jesus woke. Joseph took him, knowing he was wet, removed the wrapping, washed him, dried him, and wrapped him again. Jesus, smiling, said something that sounded like "Father." Joseph replied, "No, just Dad." Jesus repeated, "Dad." Joseph whispered, "We have much to share, more than love—life." They cuddled in the space kept for him. Joseph looked up and prayed, "Thank You." Together they slept with holy angels surrounding them, the Son of God in his arms.

Jesus woke and stirred for Mary, waking Joseph and Zena. They shifted positions to preserve warmth. Jesus, first to breakfast, relieved Joseph by saying, "Dad." Mary and Zena were moved to tears, a blend of joy and sorrow. A screeching violin woke the entire train. Soon came Himan's shouting as the wagons prepared to roll. Himan asked Joseph, "Trouble last night?" "No," Joseph replied, "only a few local boys growing up." Both moved on to their tasks, and the wagons began to roll. Zena took the reins; the horses had their fill of dew-covered grass. Daylight approached. The border would be reached before dark; they would clear the guard and continue with the escorting party. Jesus and Mary joined Zena, needing warmth together.

There was always more than enough work to do. Joseph paused at meals to be with Jesus. Jesus came to expect him. Mary and Zena were certain that the closeness between them was divinely intended. Under Joseph's guidance, Jesus developed a deep sense of mutual love and respect among people. By the time they reached Alexandria, they were finishing each other's sentences. They walked in the same steps. By the influence of the Holy Spirit, Jesus knew Joseph, and together they grew in intellect.

The day passed quickly. Himan appeared with the young and beautiful musician whose violin made men cry—Audriana Stephanotis. Zena felt jealous, but only when she saw Himan cry; she wondered if he loved Audriana. The caravan stopped for inspection out of respect for Captain Mubarek-Mubarek, a Muslim politician who had influence in securing his position. The deed granted special privilege to Himan, and all were invited to a celebration at his expense. Himan knew his strength lay in privilege. His business skills earned him honor in the world of power, a God-given advantage above others. The party lasted until morning, though the teamsters retired early enough to rest. Zena remained; she knew that if Himan were to act unwisely, she would die inside and he would lose everything—sinning against God. It was all about love within God's bonds. Jew or Muslim, business was done by the Ten Commandments given to Moses.

Morning came, and the border remained closed until the caravan was out of sight. Zena stayed with Mary and Jesus. Audriana tended to Himan's needs, accepting it as an honor that would further her career; memories of the previous night's music still stirred the emotions of many men. Jesus kept his sleep schedule and joined Joseph as the caravan departed the border. It would be a month of advancement for Jesus and his dad. Joseph knew that the power of God was never within man's reach. Jesus took his first steps at one week old, no surprise to Mary and Joseph—they had watched him climb the walls of the womb months earlier.

Joseph let Jesus walk until he reached up to be held. Joseph picked him up. "Had enough for now?" he asked. Jesus replied, "Yes," and squeezed Joseph's neck. Joseph squeezed back, and they smiled at one another. "Love one another as I love you." Later, on a stable stretch of road, Joseph set Jesus on the mule tethered to the wagon. Jesus held the mane and sat on the ridge of its spine. Joseph squeezed Jesus' hands to reassure him. Jesus rode for an hour before signaling that it was time to disembark. He returned to Mary and asked Zena, "Are you alright?" She smiled her best smile and said, "Himan is not a foolish man, nor am I a foolish woman." Joseph answered, "Temptation is always there. I give him no reason. He has earned my trust."

"Two more days to Said," Zena said. "We will establish ourselves there. The long road to Alexandria is well-traveled. A military unit will accompany us. A relative of mine, a captain, has warned us about the situation. My cousin Manes comes from an old family."

"We will celebrate the Sabbath if we arrive on time," Joseph said. "Together in one place, and together we will protect Jesus. We are of one faith, one God, through the entire journey."

Chapter 2: Jesus Ben Joseph

Jesus, teething, clung to Joseph. He held to Joseph and went to Mary only for meals. Joseph, Mary, and Zena designed a carrier for Jesus—cloth, leather, and a canvas wrap—so he could sit on Joseph's shoulders in front of his chest, facing in the same direction as Joseph. Their hands were free. Jesus listened to Joseph, copying all his mannerisms, especially in prayer. Zena said, "It is in him to be his father's son."

They were now never apart. Joseph would die for Jesus, and Mary prayed that it would never be required. She missed Jesus beside her, especially when he called her "Mary" as if practicing her name, trying to say it the way Joseph said it. Jesus was already teaching her how to be his mother as Joseph taught him how to call him Dad. Jesus would one day be a carpenter, finishing wood. Joseph spoke of it often. The art of finishing wood, he said, was like praying. When you pray, someone listens. When you finish wood, it shows you it has heard every word. Jesus rode the horse while Joseph drove by signs. Jesus learned the signs too, but the horse responded to him through kindness, as if bonded to the finish of wood. Jesus attentively considered the perspectives of those around him, refraining from judgment, seeing love as the ultimate goal of all interactions. Yet when he encountered hurt instead of love, he saw the grain of wood as pain. A fine grade of sandpaper clears the pointed edges—so what would clear the sharp edges from people? "Joseph, how does one attain forgiveness?" "From those who love you, for they give you portions of forgiveness. Collect them.

Then forgive. Those you forgive will, in turn, forgive by forgiveness. Love is born. Love is the finish of mankind." Jesus said, "Love one another as I love you—forgive one another as I forgive you."

The hardness of wood brings the finest finish. Its cellular structure, in fine increments, bonds and compresses the particles, locking the cells so there are fewer sharp edges. The long process may even take generations. Eventually, the Sabbath will open the field to all who have need, where miraculous need or calamity yields to the finest sanding, cutting away the last edges. The final lacquer seals moisture out. The awareness of mankind is the fruit of humanity's advance in the imitation of God. God makes us in God's own image, all parts and divisions of humanity included. As generations change, divisions shift from possible to probable. Time's passage introduces war, diaspora, and advances in national economies; governance turns to gold and money. Man begins to see himself as greater than God, a share-cropping governance. The advance of mankind across centuries resembles the aging of hardwood: the blending of humankind overcomes weakness that leads to death, and the lacquer becomes the resolve to life. God is the advance, for God perpetuates life. God is life, and mankind is life advancing. "Love God with all your heart, mind, and soul. Love your neighbor as yourself."

Two days passed as the sun set. The base welcomed them. Wagons circled the far end, closing off access to the military city. The rain towers were full, and showers were released. Jesus showered with Joseph. The women would shower last while the men guarded. Jesus enjoyed the sprinkle as Joseph soaped him, laughing through his first bath. Jesus said, "It is as simple as this to free your soul—just face up to God and say yes when you mean yes and no when you mean no. God will surprise us by what God already knows." Wrapped in cloth, they returned to the wagon.

Jesus and Joseph prepared the wagon for sleep. Mary and Zena cuddled for warmth as the men joined them. Mary told them they would meet the officers at dawn. After breakfast, they would begin the next part of their journey. The military would remain at the base. Jesus said to Joseph, "In the morning, I met Michael. He is here with twenty angels." He snuggled into Joseph for warmth.

They rose together, dressing while it was still dark. Jesus, in his harness, assisted Joseph with the bindings. As they mounted their horses, Michael introduced himself, telling Joseph that he and the others trained with him and twenty more every other day, two hours before advancing. "Bring Jesus along. His Father would be delighted." Joseph felt the weight of those words and nearly stumbled. "Sorry," Michael said. "I won't say that again." Daylight began the movement, and the speed doubled.

In the morning, twenty-five riders and Jesus trained just before the first wagon moved a full length.

Chapter 3: Herod Is Ill

Michael was surprised by Joseph and came to regard him as more virtuous than he had first assumed. Himan, who served in many roles, also held Michael's respect. With two women to care for, he came to train. God covered all their needs. The Son would accomplish the union of heaven and earth. Himan addressed everyone, saying, "We travel to Al-Mansaram, where three wagons will depart. The Barr families will conduct business there. I will guide them to the land where a city is to be built. I leave you in the best of hands. I will see you again in Alexandria "

The wagons advanced, accompanied by twenty-four horses with Jesus and Joseph. Their speed remained doubled. Michael saw danger ahead, and twenty riders moved to stop the oncoming horsemen. The opposing riders agreed to move aside while the wagons passed. Joseph asked Michael, "What about Herod?" Michael replied, "He has a great side, but the balance is long suffering for those who play God when they are only a king. It is said the Temple will be completed before Herod the Great passes away."

The dark hours were calm, the nights warm with a mild wind from Africa. The men worked at greasing axles. Jesus stayed with Mary, and Zena prepared to meet with Himan—a sad parting, though she was called to return to Bethlehem and live her life with him.

They would arrive ten days early. If Himan did not arrive, they would wait in the corridors stretching from the sea to the south, at the shipyards.

Joseph and Michael sought information on the Caribou Vineyards. At a tavern, they shared coffee and a tray of bread with honey; customers received information in exchange for patronage. Jesus enjoyed his first taste of bread and honey. Workers from the vineyards joined them, sharing the food and offering information. Jesus, looking much older than he was, spoke with them about grapes.

The Mancini family had come from Sicily, near the city of Messina. They had worked the grape fields in Italy. The four brothers—James, Peter, Charles, and John—lived modestly and moved to Alexandria, where they bought land and planted the grapes they had brought from Judah. Caribou gave them no history except the sea and their faith. All believed in the God of the Hebrews who had left Egypt with God's help. Their wide distribution of wine brought success. They were modest men who married modest women and trusted no one with credit.

The Turks there also believed in the one living God of Abraham. They drank Caribou wine, served it by the keg, and worked both sea and land, finding success in both. Joseph, Mary, and Jesus lived simply among them. They shared the Sabbath together, and Jesus was often sought at the sanctuary. Joseph was sought as a roofer for thatch and tile. He designed roofs and taught installation without charge. In gratitude, the community gave him a house with many windows. As a carpenter, Joseph designed shutters for all the windows to open and close easily. His cousin Zebadiah built a business crafting shutters and moved in with Joseph and Mary. Jesus grew fond of him and called him Uncle Zeb.

For three years, family and faith built a treasure of community. One people emerged from many nations. News arrived that Herod the Great had died. Joseph and Mary immediately spoke with Jesus about returning to Nazareth. Jesus understood their path would pass through Bethlehem. The family here had become the center, the core of a village that formed around Joseph and Jesus. The two were part of the community day and night, sharing meals by fire and oil lamp, welcomed into every home with a chair ready for them. The separation would be difficult. A community of many nations had built a life in the God of Moses. The well had become a sanctuary familiar and central.

A message came from Zena: Himan was at Said and would set the course of travel to Bethlehem. They were to see Leonard Goldberg, the smith near them in Alexandria. Michael knew the smith, and he and Joseph planned to travel there in daylight.

Chapter 4: Joseph And Michael

They trained that morning in the dark, Jesus with them, standing on his own and following Joseph as if they were dancing. When the training ended, Jesus returned to Mary so Joseph and Michael could discuss the details of their travel.

Joseph and Michael made their way into the inner city. Many twists and turns marked the path even in the early daylight hours. The Goldberg smith shop opened into a hall that led into the wealth of the man Michael called Len. Michael introduced Joseph as though he belonged to a kingdom of his own. Len shook Joseph's hand, blessed Michael with a broad smile, and recalled Himan as a genius. "You travel in the finest of company, integrating the past and the future. How good it is to know you. We will harbor for you a pathway for many to travel from around the world—a golden highway of everlasting life."

They entered a luxurious chamber where a great map hung from ceiling to floor. Candles illuminated the pathway to Bethlehem. Len directed them to the gold-colored markings—the little-known route of angels. Joseph and Michael studied it carefully. A woman with her face hidden brought warm, sweet wine, fresh fruit, and brandy. The three sipped brandy and tasted the dry, bitter relish made from green olives. They looked once more at the map before it scrolled upward into the ceiling, and the lights went out. Len led them back to the hallway where they had entered and wished them health above prosperity.

On the way back, Michael warned Joseph about the prosperity he had just seen. "Those who follow it are lost to the lore," he said. Then he added, "You have won me, and you will always have access to me." As they returned, darkness settled with the sweet scent of grace. Michael lifted Jesus and said, "Jesus ben Joseph." The two embraced.

Morning found them carrying out the tasks set for their departure after the Sabbath. Zebadiah shared in the partnership of the shop, which had grown into a prospering business. The house of many windows, given to Joseph and Mary, would now pass to Zebadiah along with its contents. They had arrived years ago on a mule and now left in a wagon drawn by four horses. Michael and the angels remained on horseback. The Golden Passage would take them to Said, where they would meet Himan and Zena. They would rest there for two days before continuing to Bethlehem. The travel time had been reduced by two weeks. The Golden Highway and Michael shared the honor.

They arrived at Said, weary from travel. They were housed at the Golden Inn as guests of the Goldberg family, twenty-four guests in total. The training routine and daily activities left Joseph, Jesus, and Mary exhausted by nightfall. They ate bread, fruit, wine, and water. After bathing, they gathered in the dark to share a meal of fish and vegetables. In the morning, they would dine again with Himan and Zena.

Jesus rose early, wrapped in a hooded garment on the cool morning—a gift from the priests and Rabbi Seacroft. Excited, he went in search of

Joseph and Michael, his mind filled with questions about the wealth and décor of the Inn. Joseph and Michael put him at ease, explaining that the art collection consisted of duplicates of pieces collected by the Goldberg family and gifted to the Hebrew nation. All the originals were hidden in Israel and viewed once each year, and only by those who could trace their lineage to the original flight from Egypt. Jesus admired the sling David had used to defeat the giant. Satisfied for now, he led the way to meet Himan and Zena—not for food, but for a renewal of family. As they gathered, Jesus, Mary, and Joseph touched a plane where heaven and earth seemed to meet. Meanwhile, Zena and Himan Joab celebrated the heritage of their business, their families reaching back through history to David, who replaced Saul as king. The Hebrew families blended by lineage, advancing together as rightful heirs. Their names carried a history of wealth, yet they found joy among the poor and the intellectual alike—advancing in commerce, faith, and politics.

Zena searched for Jesus, Mary, and Joseph. Seeing Mary and Joseph but failing at first to recognize Jesus—who was developing quickly both physically and intellectually—she asked, "Where is Jesus?" When Jesus answered, she burst into tears. "But he is only four!" she cried. She wrapped her arm around him, sobbing, and Joseph comforted her. She refused to leave Jesus that morning. Joseph went on to celebrate Jesus as a young tradesman, saying he would teach others carpentry when they returned to Nazareth.

Political science was a major field of study advancing business at the three universities of Said. The next day, a tour was granted of all three schools. Jesus was considered for both advanced placement and fellowship status, supported by the Goldsmith Foundation. At day's end, darkness approached as the party of seventy-one returned to dine at the Inn. The fare was light due to the hour. They would leave for Bethlehem in the morning. The Goldsmiths would see them off. There were now twenty wagons, each pulled by four horses. The loads were heavy, and Himan served again as steward.

Bethlehem was seven hours away, and Jesus was anxious to see his first home—told that it had been crowded with strangers, some self-centered and heartless, yet visited by shepherds and angels. Even the animals had provided warmth. The manger had been more than a crib. Far from poor, three kings had traveled just to see him and reveal the epiphany. Herod was gone now, and so were the babies he had murdered. Jesus, tossed between sadness and curiosity, waited to see. They passed Himan's Inn, the home and business of Himan and Zena. Jesus had been born where his earthly father was the first to see him, the first to breathe his name with love, destined to be their king even before they knew him as God—Living Word, risen over death, with a kingdom to come. Joseph would save him.

Jesus stood with Joseph and Mary. Suddenly, he seemed five years old, and tears ran down his cheeks. This was no longer his birthplace. Did his Father see him from far away or from nearby? Was his Father standing next to his dad?

Morning came, and only Michael traveled with Jesus, Mary, and Joseph. They arrived at their home and woodshop in Nazareth. Everything was as they had left it. The shop concealed the rooms, forming the quarters of their home. Jesus said, "This can be my shop. I will train my help as my dad trained me. We will fix what is broken and mend what is torn. God did this for us so we would have what we need."

Michael bent low to pick up Jesus. Jesus looked into his eyes and said, "You cannot leave us. Who will train us every other morning? I am just starting to get muscles." Suddenly, they were alone, and Joseph was holding Jesus.

Joseph and Jesus led the horses through the shop and the house to a grassy knoll behind it. They let them roam freely, for the land was fenced by neighbors. A raincatcher already stood there to water the garden and served them well. A large deciduous tree would soon provide shade as its leaves returned. A shed served as lumber storage and a tack room. All their cloth, yarn, clothing, and remedies were stored there. The wagon would deliver furniture from the shop and shutters from inventory.

The house was simple, and all three slept together for warmth in the only bed. The kitchen doubled as a catch-all. They were home—within walking distance of the sanctuary and half a day's journey from Jerusalem. The home and shop were cleaned, and neighbors came to welcome them, to help, and to meet Jesus. At day's end, bread and cheese were served. Darkness came early, and they rested. Jesus, already famous in his own quiet light, would one day be ready for his bar mitzvah, though not until he was twelve.

Business began at first light. Joseph and Jesus trained every other day, depending on purchase orders. Soon, they were a month behind. Joseph hired two men—one experienced, the other willing to train under his son. Except for Sabbath, they kept their commitments, establishing a trusted business name. Business grew, and three more men were employed and trained. In the first year, the fabrication schedule was maintained. The shop expanded, purchasing nearby homes, and the carpenters became tradesmen who repaired and rebuilt older houses. Jesus oversaw that line of work at the age of nine. The Spirit of God shaped the remaining training days, advancing him in wisdom and knowledge. At eleven, Jesus promoted the first employees to leadership, teaching them to own their responsibilities and guide others. This was the "yes" Jesus gave to his Father.

Life continued in familiar rhythms. Joseph was under investigation for the incident involving the soldier who had laid hands on Mary. The soldier had taken his own life due to alcohol poisoning, and the accusation was reduced to an investigation. A team of four men pursued the matter, but Joseph felt confident he would be cleared. Labor-intensive work filled every day except the Sabbath, the only lawful day of rest.

The next morning, Michael knocked, alerting them. Jesus opened the door with a smile, but Michael, alarmed, grabbed Joseph's arm. He asked Jesus to answer another knock at the door. Avoiding Mary, Michael pulled

Joseph through the shop and into the animal garden—then vanished with him.

Moments later, the door opened again, and the guards entered, asking for Joseph. They were led through the shop and into the yard. Finding no one, they appeared confused. Unable to locate him, they left at once, saying to Jesus, "Tell your dad we are looking for him."

"The four celebrations were planned for the end of the week to mark the beginning of adult life and responsibility. Jesus and John, who loved Joseph deeply, were to live as sons to him and to Mary. Joseph now lived in everlasting life as a guest of Michael the Archangel. Jesus would not live by earthly power, for the power of God belongs to God alone. Jesus would rise from the dead, and those who know him would be resurrected before returning to everlasting life. By the resurrection of Christ, the gates of hell and heaven opened. Jesus would await Mary, who would take the chair at the left hand of the Father. At the right hand of Mary would be the Holy Spirit. At the left hand of the Father would be the Son. Joseph would partner with Michael the Archangel, and together they would train every other day, Jesus with them. The Father advances all children. In free will, all may become God's children, resolving to be in the likeness of Jesus, who never said no to the Father. If I do not become Jesus, I will ask to be this Joseph."

JOE P. MESSINA.

24